PURCELL

Come ye Sons of Art

Ode for the birthday of Queen Mary 1694
arranged for SSA & piano

by MAURICE BLOWER

Order No: NOV 070355

NOVELLO PUBLISHING LIMITED

FOREWORD

This ode, a tribute for Queen Mary's birthday, in 1694, was originally written for SATB chorus, oboes, trumpets, timpani and strings. This arrangement brings a charming work within the reach of female voice choirs.

The Overture and some of the Ritornelli have been omitted. A version of the accompaniment for piano and strings is available on hire from the publishers.

M.B.

Duration 15 minutes

COME YE SONS OF ART

Ode for the Birthday of Queen Mary 1694

Arranged for SSA and Piano
by MAURICE BLOWER

HENRY PURCELL

Come, come, ye Sons__ of Art, Come, come, a__ way,_____ Come, come, ye

Sons__ of Art, Come, come, a - way,_____ Tune all__ your voi - ces,__ and

19516

in - stru - ments play, To ce-le-brate, to ce-le-brate this tri - um - phant day.

27

Tune all your voi - ces, and in - stru - ments play, To ce-le-brate, to ce-le-brate this

33

tri - um - phant day, to ce-le-brate, to ce-le-brate this tri - um - phant day.

39

SOPRANO I

Come, come, ye Sons_ of Art, Come, come, a - way, Come, come, ye Sons_ of Art,

SOPRANO II

Come, come, ye Sons of Art, Come, come, a - way,_____ Come, come, ye Sons of Art,

ALTO

Come, come, ye Sons_ of Art, Come, come, a - way,_____ Come, come, ye Sons_ of Art,

45

4

tri - um - phant day, To ce - le-brate, to ce - le-brate this tri - um - phant day.

tri - um-phant day, To ce - le-brate, to ce - le-brate this tri - um - phant day.

tri - um-phant day, To ce - le-brate, to ce - le-brate this tri - um - phant day.

67

SOUND THE TRUMPET

Allegro moderato

SOPRANO I

Sound

SOPRANO II, ALTO

Allegro moderato

the trum - pet,

Sound the

4

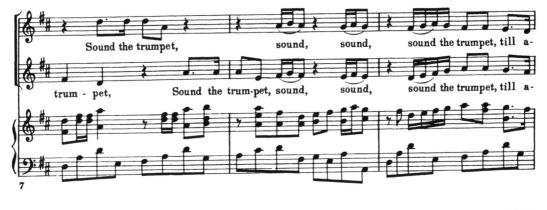

Sound the trumpet, sound, sound, sound the trumpet, till a-

trum - pet, Sound the trum-pet, sound, sound, sound the trumpet, till a-

7

round

round You make the list-'ning shores re - bound,

10

You make the list-'ning shores re - bound, re - bound,

You make the list-'ning shores re - bound,

12

the list-'ning shores re - bound.

You make the list-'ning shores re - bound.

14

num - bers can em - ploy, To ce - le - brate, to ce - le -

can ____ em-ploy, To ce - le - brate, to ce - le -

26

brate ____ the glo - ries of _ this day, the glo -

brate ____ the glo - ries of _ this _ day, the

28

_ ries, the glo - - - - - - - - - - - - -

glo - - - ries, the glo - - - - - -

30

- - - ries of this day.

- - - ries of this day. On the day.

32

STRIKE THE VIOL

harp, in - spire _____ the flute, wake __ the harp, in -

harp, in - spire the flute, wake __ the

spire _____ the flute. flute.

harp, in - spire the flute. flute. Sing your pa - tron -

sing your pa - tron - ess - es praise, sing,

ess - es praise, sing your pa - tron-ess-es praise, sing,

sing, sing, sing, In_ cheer - ful, in_ cheer - - ful,

sing, sing, sing,___ In_ cheer - - ful, in_ cheer -

32

in_ cheer - - -ful and har - mon - ious lays. lays.

- -ful, in cheer-ful and har - mon - ious lays. lays.

37

poco rall.

poco rall.

42

THE HONOUR OF A JUBILEE

have, let it, let it have, let it have the hon - our of a Ju - bi - lee.

have, let it, let it have, let it have the hon - our_ of a Ju - bi - lee.

have, let it, let it have, let it have the hon - our of a Ju - bi - lee.

35

BID THE VIRTUES

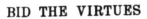

Adagio

SOPRANO I (or Oboe solo)

Bid the Vir - tues, bid the Gra -

SOPRANO II

Bid the Vir - tues, bid the Gra - - ces,

Adagio

- ces To the sa - - - - - -

bid the Gra-ces To the sa - - - -

4

14

THESE ARE THE SACRED CHARMS

- - - - - - tal pow'r she draws, Thus,—

pow'r, im - mor - - - tal pow'r she draws, to his aid im - mor -tal pow'r, to his

30

thus, thus_____ to his aid im - mor - - -

aid im - mor -tal pow'r, to his aid im - mor - - - - tal

32

poco rall.

- - - - - - - - tal pow'r she draws.

pow'r,_____ to his aid im-mor -tal pow'r, im - mor - tal pow'r she draws.

poco rall.

34

SEE NATURE, REJOICING

laugh - ing vale, re - ply - ing hill,

laugh - ing vale, re - ply - ing hill,

laugh - ing vale, re - ply - ing hill, With charm - ing

17

The hap - py sea - son

The hap - py sea - son

har - mo - ny___ u - nite, The hap - py sea - son

22

to in - vite. Thus Na - ture, re - joic - ing, has shown us___ the

to in - vite. Thus Na - ture, re - joic - ing, has shown us the

to___ in - vite. Thus Na - ture, re - joic - ing, has shown us the

27

Na - ture, re - joic - ing, has shown us__ the way, With in - no - cent

Na - ture, re - joic - ing, has shown us the way, With in - no - cent

Na - ture, re - joic - ing, has shown us the way, With in - no - cent

47

re - vels to wel - come the__ day.

re - vels to wel - come the day.

re - vels, with in - no - cent re - vels to wel - come the day.

52

poco rall.

poco rall.

57

Printed and bound in Great Britain by
Caligraving Limited Thetford Norfolk